JEN HADFIELD is a poet and visual artist living in Shetland. Her first collection, *Almanacs*, won an Eric Gregory Award in 2003 and her second, *Nigh-No-Place*, won the T. S. Eliot Prize in 2008, making her the youngest female poet to receive the award. Her Picador collections are *Byssus*, published in 2014, and *The Stone Age*, winner of the Highland Book Prize in 2022. Jen Hadfield's prose memoir *Storm Pegs: A Life Made in Shetland* appeared from Picador in 2024. She is a 2024 recipient of a Windham Campbell Prize for her poetry.

ALSO BY JEN HADFIELD

Poetry

Almanacs

Nigh-No-Place

Byssus

The Stone Age

Prose

Storm Pegs: A Life Made in Shetland

Jen Hadfield

Selected Poems

PICADOR

First published 2025 by Picador
an imprint of Pan Macmillan
The Smithson, 6 Briset Street, London EC1M 5NR
EU representative: Macmillan Publishers Ireland Ltd, 1st Floor,
The Liffey Trust Centre, 117–126 Sheriff Street Upper,
Dublin 1, D01 YC43
Associated companies throughout the world
www.panmacmillan.com

ISBN 978-1-0350-3285-3

Almanacs originally published 2005 by Bloodaxe Books.
Nigh-No-Place originally published 2008 by Bloodaxe Books.
Byssus first published 2014 by Picador.
The Stone Age first published 2021 by Picador.

1 3 5 7 9 8 6 4 2

A CIP catalogue record for this book is available from the British Library.

Printed and bound in Great Britain by Bell & Bain Ltd, Glasgow

for Mum and Dad

Contents

from *Almanacs*

Melodeon on the Road Home 3

Saturnalia 4

Strath Ossian 6

XIV Temperance 7

Crying Taing 8

Iamb 9

Orchid Dog 10

Dog-days 11

Full Sheeptick Moon 12

Song of Parts 14

0 The Fool – Skye 15

from *Nigh-No-Place*

Nigh-No-Place 19

The Mandolin of May 21

Lucky Seven 25

Dipper 26

The Blokes and the Beasties 27

Avenue Zero 28

Kodachrome 30

A Bad Day for Icefishing 31

Prenatal Polar Bear 32
Paternoster 33
Ladies and Gentlemen This Is a Horse as Magritte Might Paint Him 34
Odysseus and the Sou'wester 35
Glid 37
Self-portrait as a Fortune-telling Miracle Fish 38
Ten-minute Break Haiku 39
Daed-traa 40
The Wren 42
Love's Dog 43
Teatros 44
In the Same Way 46
Cabbage 47

from *Byssus*

Lichen 51
Smiles learnt in the cockle-beds 52
We climb the hill in the dark and the children are finally given back their iPhones 54
The Kids 56
The Ambition 58
To be benthic 60
Hydra 61
Manure 63

Olick 64
Da Coall 66
Puffballs 69
The Plinky-Boat 72
The Jellyfish 74
from Definitions 75
Five Mackerel 78
The Moult 80
from Hairst 81
A Very Circular Song 83

from *The Stone Age*

After Vestey's Well 87
Granny Whose Gaze 88
Wild Garlic 90
Skunk Cabbage 91
Umbrella 92
Oyea 93
Dolmen 94
Hardanger Fiddle & Nyckelharpa 96
Shadow 98
Rhubarb 100
Swans 102
Rockpool 103
Nudibranch 104

Limpet 106
Ert-fast 108
Strimmer 110
Nettles 111
First Draft 112

ACKNOWLEDGEMENTS 115

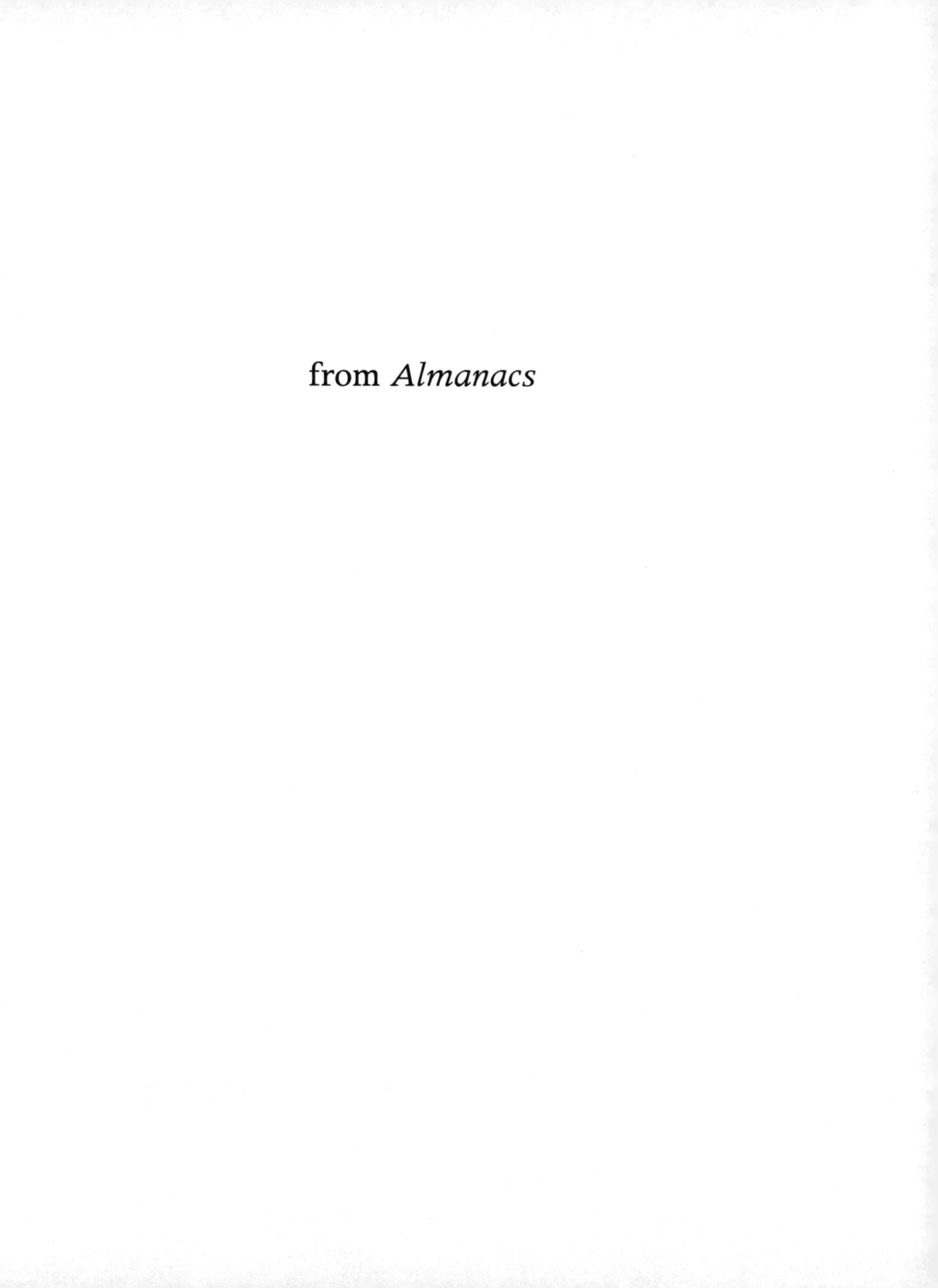

from *Almanacs*

Melodeon on the Road Home

for Jenny

I love your slut dog,
as silent with his three print spots
as a musical primer.
He sags like a melodeon
across my spread knees.
When I dig my fingers
into the butterfly hollows
in his chest, he pushes my breasts
apart with stiff legs.
Isn't it good
to forget you're anything but fat
and bone? I'm telling you
it's good to be hearing your dog's tune
on the broad curve out of town,
a poem starting,
pattering the breathless little keys.
To see more than me, I flick
the headlamps to high beam
and it's as if I pulled an organ stop –
black light wobbling
in the wrinkles of the road,
high angelus of trees.

Saturnalia

i

She can't wait to cross
the barbed wire.

Resurrection of the Green Knight!
Green floods her, gloom welshes her.

Her numb fingers
are buzzing with plankton.

ii

Her stick stabs mulch
as deep as snow; she drops
it, hangs on holly to cut holly.

iii

She wears small wounds for weeks,
a bruise lashed to her leg like a flint to a spear.

iv

Pie-eyed with danger,
a pantomime burglar,
she banishes me
to distant scant-berried trees.

v

I can't remember
the last time
I was in a wood.

Strath Ossian

So on down the strath, a dark hill and a bright mountain and between the two that old dervish is stirring up clouds, with a cracked bit of antler from skirmishes of last spring. A right good mood he's in, grinning like a burst dam, and everything rumpus: the pan lid chittering, the tea meths-scented. His sour little teeth crack the last Pink Lady. If he doesn't watch it he'll get kissed, just for the sake of the bright hill, the dark mountain, the drinking bitter tea

well what was I meant to do? Kiss that quartzy boulder?

XIV Temperance

Harmonics – a starling
whistling, diode skylark
scrolling radio stations

sheep speaking the New Lamb
condensed black shadow
of his white dam.

You have to move more slowly
round the small moment
you have to move more small-ly.

The anchor rope plumb
from his belly
the blood rust beneath the tail.

Tinily constellations creep the night
and I orbit the still ewe
and her upwards-butting moon.

Crying Taing

The peat is cherried with thick water.
I lever out bones like almonds.
From the grass I pick bones like butterflies
with moor-coloured bone-circled eyes.

From bones like orchids, pan-pipes, fans,
I build the ewe kicking out last night at cars
and the small leap of Ronas Voe;
today blood-muzzled, blind.

I pick up a fragment
for every bone in my body.
My fingers as cold as the bones in the grass.
I wind them round a panhandle, a pen.

Iamb

And when in days or weeks the wind drops,

I'll give up my raggedy herding

walk warm and slow along the road, gathered about by breath.

Let it veer under the rusted tractor.

Let it return, lamb-shadow, butting.

Canter ahead of my slow step.

And when the wind drops, my ears will lose their squint wings.

I'll flinch for no skua or passing car.

There'll be no waking   exhausted from flying,

my good silt marrow settled home in bone again.

Each hill take on again its load.

The moor billow a sheet of birds.

Orchid Dog

Orchid Dog swells at dusk,
claiming the clapboard moor,
its chambered cairns and basalt topknots.

He raises a field-full of white gulls,
shadow bruising a bloated sheep.
He jerks and swings a mouthful of rank ribbons.

Orchid Dog is soaked and shoulder-deep.
The burn hanks his hair, bares
his belly-suede and coded nipples.

He hunts a flooded vole
he'll never kill and polkas on it
jumping on and off its hot ember.

I scuff wet grasses for a rock anvil.
He rolls the wet plush
in the rose and chocolate corals of his grin.

Dog-days

There was and there wasn't a summer and it hung half-clipped from the mountain's scraped shoulders. Sun just a stain, a fleecy stain. Months ago, the tup.

In the Cuillin, an old rescue dog chafes its wet neck on Sgurr nan Gillean. It's Skerryman's hound, cross between a haar and a husky. He found it locked in a transit van, shit and a dead sheep, coat matted to daub and wattle. Three Days, *Good Dog*, not barking.

There was and there wasn't a summer when the mountains were like stone-chipped teeth. And Skerryman's finger, unhooked from the soft gape, let cloud furl up to heal the hurt gums. *And if the dog's not died, they're still there now.*

Full Sheeptick Moon

Weedy drymouth Feb
– Les Murray 'Feb'

An hour at high-tide,
edgy patience with the fankle-line
of July, bail-arm jammed,
hooks gripped in the grind.

A ribbon teaseweed
to flutter my spinner,
greenly.

*

Dimps of season July,
new dot to dot galaxies of freckle,
clear dabs of midge honey;

July, our sun
in wee wet bursts
that bless the heads of orchids'
ragatag magenta.

A raised red season
but nerveless as the quenched wine-glasses.

Woke at four to their fingerprints
and pale mouths, a tremulous
cooling hour,

watching the lighthouse
smear the haar.

*

Now summer is the season
of clingings-on, high dithering grasses,
this-an-that of mackerel.

Summer sky peeled from your soles
in grey crescents.

The swallows come, wings
black boomerang,
loaded with ticks
and pearly winter weathers.

Song of Parts

This is how the catch is gutted –
you diddle the knife down fatty silver,
fingernail-deep, the broad blade's tip.
Slow burgundies stain the enamel sink.
Mackerel hoop and harden in your grip.
With tugsome bravery you yank
the gut-end, coda of a bloodless old song;
the silty fruits coddled away;
the clean fish and its swimbladder,
like a tigerlily,
                    on the cutting board

0 The Fool – Skye

May you find your spraints of claw
and coiled damp tail and splintered bone
and brochs of snails and seeds of fruits
          all fortune-cookied.

May the light land
every day differently on your bird-table

mackerel black

                                        mackerel silver

from *Nigh-No-Place*

Nigh-No-Place

I prithee, let me bring thee where crabs grow;
And I with my long nails will dig thee pignuts . . .
– The Tempest

I will meet you at Pity Me Wood.
I will meet you at Up-To-No-Good.

I will meet you at Stank, Shank and Stye.
I will meet you at Blowfly.

I will meet you at Low Spying How.
I will meet you at Salt Pie.

I will meet you at Coppertop.
I will meet you at Scandale Bottom.

I will meet you at Crackpot Moor.
I will meet you at Muker.

I will meet you at Dirty Piece.
I will meet you at Booze, Alberta.

I will meet you at Bloody Vale.
I will meet you at Hunger Hill.

I will bring you to New Invention.
I will bring you to Lucky Seven.

I will bring you from Shivery Man.
I will bring you to The Lion and Lamb.

I will bring you to the North Light.
I will bring you to Quiet-the-Night.

I will bring you to Hush.
I will bring you to Hungry Hushes.

I will bring you to Grace, Alberta.
I will bring you to Nigh-No-Place.

I will meet you at Two O'Clock Creek.
Will you go with me?

The Mandolin of May

Twas in the merry month of May,
when the green buds were swellin . . .
– Barbry Allen

Big maples and at the end of the lane, the garden bursts open like a dropped melon. Mealy mash of appletrees, hacked wet chunk of mountain.

I carry the chamber pot from casita to bathroom. My hems drag in the wet grass. Cottonseed roils and sinks slowly, cladding the roof and catching on the gutter like curds.

What the muggy mountain says. 'I beat my breast, thumped my brother, pulled him to my chest. Roll them down.'

His gold teeth are radiant, a trove of sullen ore; the sweat runs from his skull to collar. Pouring from the car, the air-conditioned air curdles.

I'm no great shakes at babies but I've been thinking more and more about mandolins, as the weeks go by. Crumpled notes would prang out of those paired strings, a salvage-metal sound, like freight cars screeling over a crossing.

I'd squash a chord, dent a bumper. Manage a grace-note, like a rock-chip ticking off the windscreen. Notes clip off the pick like grasshoppers off a dumped washer-dryer, in the milky sun, blotted out with wildfire, in Tsiigehchic.

Ping, pang. Every string would have its twin.

If I had a mandolin, I'd hug it to my belly like a watermelon.

A cobweb strains against my shoulder. I cradle the long lens on a bough.

I step right out into chipping sound, wet daylight and the river roar. I totter to the river, like a deer or drunken bridegroom.

A slow-worm writhes like a parched old ampersand; a fisherman cuddles a broad swathe of silver. On every spinner he lands a salmon – a Chinook – a thirty-pound Springer.

Gravel popping on the drive – a visitor with hopeful eyes, and a potted daisy in a brown paper bag. Come back at five and you'll get your bloody hospitality.

My river – warm shallows – rocks and gumbo mud, fish soup and dumplings. The glacial rapids – mine, mine like an ice-cream headache.

Rockhound, I pat hot plutons like favourite nags.

The same spoiled poem over and over; mushy round the peach-pit of the poem before. The same commas maul it, like fruitflies.

The famous flood at Elsa's place, when a cedar jackknifed and tore out a quarter-acre, a Fauve sweep of sand and unanimous water.

With the white eye of a prophet, the salmon unravels but swims upriver.

The gabardine mountain pegged up in rain, drooling dye like a pinafore.

Lock the toolshed, strip the bed in the casita, shake the clinging seeds, grass, faint hairs from the Hudson Bay blanket. The fetid residual warmth of a nest.

I start the last load in the dishwasher and then find the buttered knife and compost bowl; sagging potatoes; cold handful of gravy.

Grandmère tonsures a tomato with a sharp little knife. She saws around the withered stalk, excising the sunken socket. On her way to the compost, she offers herself the tomato in her palm, as if she were the horse.

All the way up the lane, tyres lumping over ruts and sinkholes, a robin runs ahead like a pageboy.

Larry's cat is twenty years old and some kinda sage: deep-keeled like a sacred ox, with punka belly and swaying skinny hindquarters.

Grandmère shows which fields are planted with corn. I don't see anything coming.

As she operates the slicer, the girl's butt wags like a hornet's. Bacon accumulates in her palm like insoles.

Grandmère sets down her tumbler. Ice-cubes clank in rye and water. *I thought I heard a bell*, she says. I show the glass, shake it. I say it sounds like the bloody cows coming home.

Lucky Seven

There is no hogging the secret stations in the night – Capreol, Sioux Lookout, Lucky Seven. Anyone who wakes wakes a wave of blurred anemones, that sit up and see with closed eyes. Engineers' huts, sidings, halfhour station-stops where passengers totter to smoke and shiver and scuff the dull rails. Sidetracked for freight, our sickish slowing in the dark. We sleep with necks apparently broken across headrests and armrests, however we manage to pile our bones. Nancy's feet are sweetbreads in thick white socks that crowd my seat. Who goes under first? I can hear her breathing breaking. She chuckles, and chokes on chuckle in her sleep, the sheet of air between carriage and freightcars thumping like a wobbleboard. I sleep. I wake. I sleep. I wake. Nancy comes in cold and stale from the Miramichi fag break –

Dipper

he goes on – *so I said to the guy I saw a bear here last year and aw, jings, did it ever smell bad* – I said how, he says – *you know, like a polecat, or a ferret hutch: aw* –

and I've a momentary out-of-body experience, the dark outside the headlamps driving Chilliwack River Road, a word ('fishy') in my head, then tumble back into this monologue like a dipper and run along the riverbed with roaring ears

and as he said up at the salmon hatchery when the Coho are spawning the dippers just tip right into the river and grab a single egg and jump out of the water with it in their beak and brrr! they just shake (he shudders) *and they're dry* –

The Blokes and the Beasties

I defy noctiphobia to watch the summer constellations rise, and name for the first time the blokes and the beasties – Leo, the kite of Libra, Virgo's long torso, the Huntsman Boötes. The blimp Ophiuchus is a cross between a python and a manatee, Serpens Caput to Serpens Cauda. Satellites score the sky as tiny bubbles crawl up a glass of cola. Had I reached the wilderness I would see yet more shuddering stars, clinging to the strapping constellations like greenfly. Kyoots or wolves are shouting in the black flames of poplars. I am backed up against the porch door with all the lights off, a torch just to find the handle. I'm scared of seeing something Big; they say moose, wattled like jigsaw pieces, emanate in the halflight. And yet I sleep on my belly, under the bent knee and flexed bicep of the big man, Hercules –

Avenue Zero

On Avenue Zero the blueberry is king
and blow thrives in roadside ditches.

We share our border with a superpower
and the ditches are flooded with stagnant water.

We were farm-folk, we are neighborhood watch.
We build on the precipice. We build on the floodplain.

We build where skunk cabbage flowered in April.
We build where Dutch farmers once

cut drooling daffodils, and their spittle whirled
on the wind like lassos.

We buy up the honey farms and we build on the land
below the broken tines of the windbreak.

On Avenue Zero spring's overdue.
The mountain wears its snowpack high and heavy.

A heron trolls a dry puddle
and hummers arrive before blossoms have set.

On Avenue Zero the birds can't settle.
We fear the pathological flus.

The frail farm cottages
burst like seedpods.

We stump and we dynamite and
we build in the orchards.

Tall horses sway in a handkerchief pasture.
Our mansions emulate the summits of Mount Zero.

Kodachrome

Thirty years back, in the Cariboo, Grandmère highstepped the creek, crushing pussywillow to her chest, a bouquet of cagoules.

Your shirt was plaid: red and blue. It *cleared* your belly, thirty years back, in the Cariboo.

Grandmère scraped a firepit with the side of her foot.

You dragged a canoe.

James and Moira ran off for wood. You'd told them to shout – *heybear, heybear* – and did they ever –

Hey bear!

Hey bear!

A godawful wriggly thing fell in Moira's hair.

Moira got a frog in a stranglehold and James, naked, crushed his cowboy hat against his head.

In the sunrise, your plaid shirt practically bled.

Snow still huddled under some of the pines like lambs.

The fields wore cows like fuzzy Hombergs.

Behind, a herd of astounded hills.

A Bad Day for Icefishing

The tyres creep onto the scab of the lake
and there we are – walking on water.

Smoke-rings clatter from the gas-powered motor.
A wormcast of ice slumps from the augur

and over our fishing-hole we bunch like bears,
sift gristly water through a slotted spoon.

We rig the bait – the curled grub and lure –
winch them tenderly down the twinkling fathoms,

stroll them across the wasted lakefloor,
while stealthy, the hole in the ice heals over.

A bad day for fish?
But white noise fogs our lungs and our line.

Your dog makes angels
in the piled banks of snow.

Prenatal Polar Bear

He hangs in formaldehyde
like a softmint or astronaut
dreaming in his moonsuit –
a creased, white world.

His paws are opalescent
and dinted with seedclaws –
the flattened, unripe,
strawberries-of-the-snows.

Paternoster

Paternoster. Paternoster.
Hallowed be thy mane.
Thy kingdom come.
Thy draftwork be done.
Still plough the day
And give out daily bray
Though heart stiffen in the harness.
Then sleep hang harness with bearbells
And trot on bravely into sleep
Where the black and the bay
The sorrel and the grey
And foals and bearded wheat
Are waiting.
It is on earth as it is in heaven.
Drought, wildfire,
Wild asparagus, yellow flowers
On the flowering cactus.
Give our daily wheat, wet
Whiskers in the sonorous bucket.
Knead my heart, hardened daily.
Heal the hoofprint in my heart.
Give us our oats at bedtime
And in the night half-sleeping.
Paternoster. Paternoster.
Hallowed be thy hot mash.

Ladies and Gentlemen This Is a Horse as Magritte Might Paint Him

Consider this percheron in the climate-
controlled hold, gimped up for the flight
in blinkers and bridle and drugged of course
from the creased Jupiter of his arse
to the spotted dominoes of his teeth,
the burden of his blood alone,
the clapper seized in his brain's bell,
propped up on steel and the air's goodwill.
Ladies and Gentlemen – will you fill your glasses?
May I lead us all in a toast or prayer?
May the horse never wake
that stands in mid-air

the horse never wake that stands in

mid-air

horse never wake that stands in

mid-air

Odysseus and the Sou'wester

When Odysseus and his crew left his island, the King, Aeolus, made him a final present – a fine breeze for the journey and the leather haversack in which the rest of the winds were imprisoned, warning him not to open the bag. Guess what . . .

I caught and oxtered it like a rugby ball,
a bloated bell of beating leather,
and for weeks I nannied the bloody thing –
on my lap, mending sails,
in a papoose, to climb the rigging.
When the boys got steamed on Aeolian wine,
I cuddled my squirming supper of winds,
let no one spell me for a wink of sleep.
From Aeolus to Malea was a waking dream.
Fat kingcups wobbled like boxing gloves.
With open eyes, I dreamt of home.
I clicked my heels in the blinking squill,
pillowed my skull on my second head,
and the boys said,
*oo*mpa-pa
*oo*mpa-pa,
Rockabye Baby!
as I dandled us home
on the sweet vesper gale.

*

Now the low, brown island strains on tiptoes,
and fences are strung with trembling streamers,
and the sea's mad as milk.

And my cheeks are scored with milky tears.
And like a puffball bursts the bag of winds.

And there's the Sou'wester,
a rising loaf of ruffled feathers,
struggling from the haversack
like a furious swan.

Glid

I turn the camera on my dissolving self,
pale-tongued and rabbit-eyed –

I turn the camera on dazzled
Everything –

plain rain – the loch –
the incandescent horses

forged black against the broch –
me, my brimming head,

precarious as a dandelion clock –
and dimpling the loch,

black button on bright,
a dinghy row-rowed,

skewered with light.

Self Portrait as a Fortune-telling Miracle Fish

I'm disappointed in the gods that formed me thus
in the likeness of the wall-eyed Halibut;
in my longing, a Meagre or Eelpout;
in my maudlin, a Poor Cod or Bitterling.

I'm disgusted with whichever of you
chose jealousy-with-an-overbite
to be my consort, my symbiotic groupie

and yet some rogue demi-deity
gave a posy of dubious virtues –
made me transparent; electric;

a Wide-eyed Flounder; a Crystal Gobi;
a Stargazer; a Velvet-belly;
a Deepsea Angler, blind

were it not for this proboscis
that lets me troll my little lantern
in the silt and dim
off the continental shelf.

And my daemon's a dogfish – I think –
a Starry Hound, a blunt and hungry hobo,
scrounging, starveling, sleeping on the go.

Ten-minute Break Haiku

Just the blades prattling
on cartilage – cut here, here –
a good, fat fillet.

*

My friend the Cuckoo
Wrasse, hauled from his dark holler,
wilting on ice. Alas.

*

Breading haddock, I
bury in the coarse, bright dunes
the pale, wet children.

*

I finger the cur-
ious, quilted sphincter, being
like this, inside, too.

*

Gut-worms, Christ! Still I
pluck them from the membranes,
one by one.

Daed-traa

I go to the rockpool at the slack of the tide
to mind me what my poetry's for.

It has its ventricles, just like us –
pumping brine, like bull's blood, a syrupy flow.

It has its theatre –
hushed and plush.

It has its Little Shop of Horrors.
It has its crossed and dotted monsters.

It has its cross-eyed beetling Lear.
It has its billowing Monroe.

For monks, it has barnacles
to sweep the broth as it flows, with fans,
grooming every cubic millimetre.

It has its ebb, the easy heft of wrack from rock,
like plastered, feverish locks of hair.

It has its *flodd*.
It has its welling god
with puddled, podgy face and jaw.

It has its holy hiccup.

Its minute's silence

daed-traa.

I go the rockpool at the slack of the tide
to mind me what my poetry's for.

The Wren

for V.

This will be your last life here. I see a dropsy helicopter, choring along. A heron like a sickle reaps an Iron-Age sun. I see the Caravan. You've been travelling on your own but – Dear God – like falling face down into warm mud, this is love – the sudden, muddy sun.

You have the Polytunnel. Something about you will need protecting. A bust creel's a debt. You have a debt . . . doesn't every-one? Money is a pile of anything. Cabbages mean money as manure does. Cool leaves creak between your palms in the evening. It's enough. Pull one.

I see the Wren. Behind and before, above and below you. That's luck. And under the sun, the Dark-Haired Hammerer. In the gleaming grass, the ducks will gleam like curling stones. You'll get off scot-free, trusting everyone.

You will love the land. You will love the land like a bairn. The Hammerer. The Wren. The dropsy helicopter choring along. The heron like a sickle reaps an Iron-Age sun.

Love's Dog

after Edwin Morgan

What I love about love is its diagnosis
What I hate about love is its prognosis

What I hate about love is its me me me
What I love about love is its Eat-me/Drink-me

What I love about love is its petting zoo
What I love about love is its zookeeper – you

What I love about love is its truth serum
What I hate about love is its shrinking potion

What I love about love is its doubloons
What I love about love is its bird-bones

What I hate about love is its boil-wash
What I love about love is its spin-cycle

What I loathe about love is its burnt toast and bonemeal
What I hate about love is its bent cigarette

What I love about love is its pirate
What I hate about love is its sick parrot

Teatros

for R

Jellyfish

Medusae – babes
in the wood, with milky domes
and faint fontanelles;

constellations that
someone shook into the sea,
orphan circlet of

fangs, spasming; a
mussed map of heavens, thimbles
on the tide, all thumbs.

Dénouement

Across the rockpool's frilled theatre,
a limpet budges
a devastating millimetre

Nature Study

Salted tapwater – she knits it
with puzzled antennae;
then from her shell

unpacks a banana bunch of claws,
her googly green haversack of roe,
and last – fascination and woe –

a trailing corkscrew quiff of tail,
a soft nought –
her kernel.

In the same way

In the same way she cries at the kitchen door
and I slip her and she runs into circular squalls of rain

and she cries at the kitchen door
with snailtracks of rain in her muscular fur
so I open up, and she runs in singing

and she cries at the kitchen door
so I open up and she crouches
then sprints into the wind

and the wind cries at the kitchen door
so I open up and call and call

and she doesn't run in but the wind does,
with rain, a squall of claws –

in the same dogged, idiotic way
I open up, send Goodnight across the brae,

and the wind canters in
and she with a wild carol

and all the night hail
melted gleaming in her furs

Cabbage

I ask the garden to bear me witness
but what the ground offers as evening comes
looks most of all like a snoozing face –
whorled, shut, deaf to disgrace –
a mute Om from a drill of Oms,
cool leaves creaking – a Northern lotus.

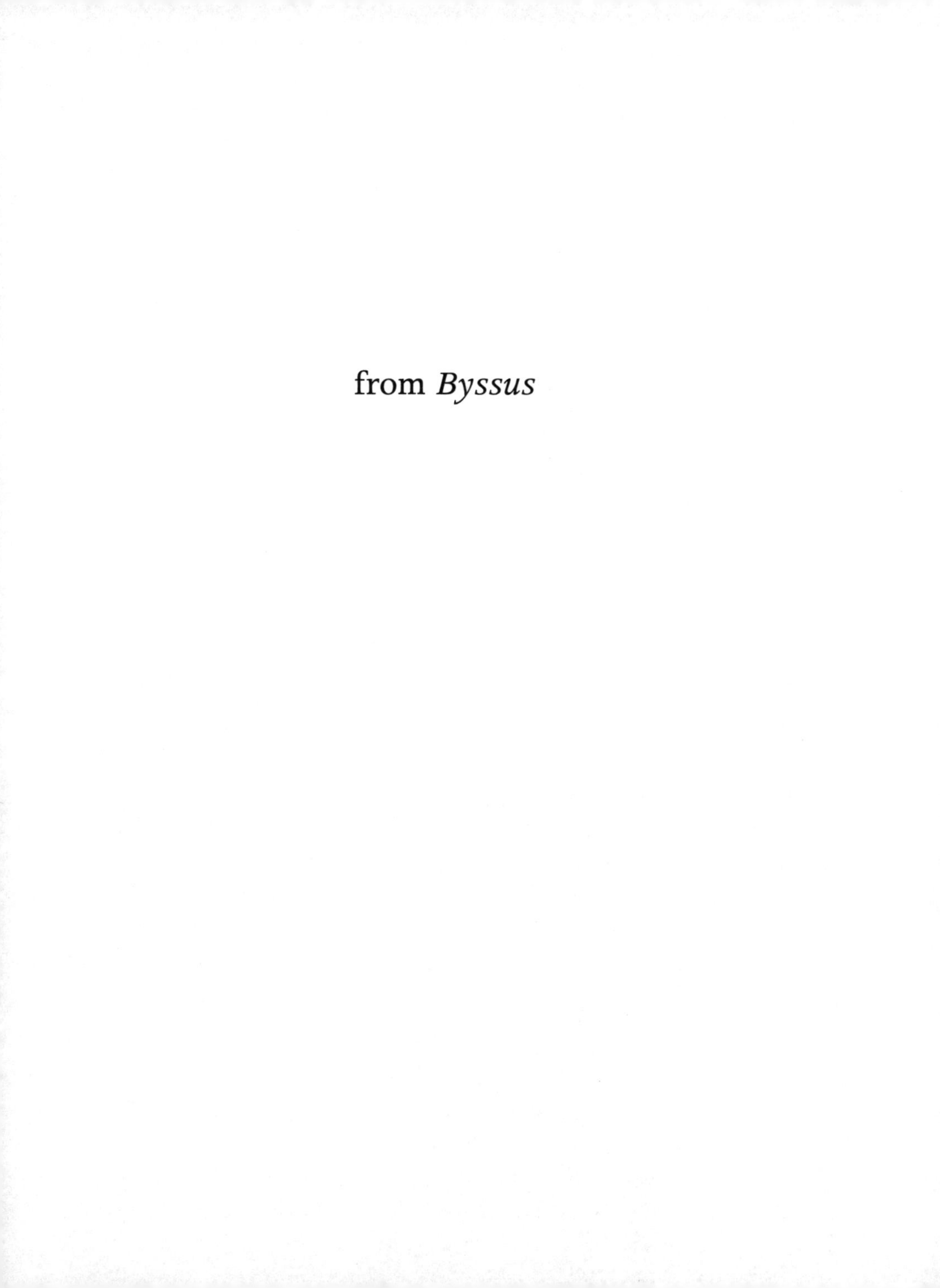

from *Byssus*

Lichen

Who listens
like lichen listens

assiduous millions of black
and golden ears?

You hear

                    and remember

but I'm speaking
to the lichen.

The little ears prunk,
scorch and blacken.

The little golden
mouths gape

the cockle's smile

Smiles learnt in the cockle-beds

is an ambiguous
smile

a brackish
smile

a sidling
smile

a conservative
smile

a dole
smile

a self-centred
smile

a stuck-in-the-
mud smile

a salad-days
smile

a gummy
smile

a scare-yourself
smile

a spit-in-your
eye smile

a tough-nut-
to-crack smile

a philosopher-
waving-his-quodlibet-
of-wrack smile

a Smeagol
smile

a survival
smile

a final
smile

a fossil

smile

We climb the hill in the dark and the children are finally given back their iPhones

. . . mid-sentence, Kusra,
bravening, detaches
her humid paw
from mine, swept up

like a ripened copepod
in a current of complaint
and omniscient
App-light. To avert

the dirty, natural night
they've cracked open
their phones like geodes:
dazzled we stream

through the wedged ruts
and cowpats, fishing
for a signal or satellite.
Mum! I'm safe, I've got

six bars. Shaniya
touched egg-blood! Miss –
get back into the line
of light! And finally

attempt to take pics
of the stars, of dark
country lanes, of the hot
perturbation of Sirius.

The Kids

Born too soon,
Monday's child was unready to be seen;
is destined to be early for ever.

She's selected a slice of red pepper
shaped
like a question mark.

*

The volcanic breath of Tuesday's child!
He remembers where poetry comes from;
the literal potential of things,

which means he can't eat broccoli –
seeing it right, a tiny indigestible oak.

He eats grated cheese with a teaspoon,
assisting it with a finger.

*

The hidden's the vocation of bird-like Wednesday's child,
perfecting her dust-baths with sweeping boughs of pine.

She can find anything hidden in the dark,
as a cat finds a rabbit –

by steam escaping
the warren.

*

Thursday's child says he saw Wednesday's child
run so fast she began to fly.

Thursday's child shall be called a liar.

*

Friday is afraid of the suit of spades
and jigsaw pieces the shape of the suit of spades.

She's afraid of plug-sockets, pylons,
dams, flowered wallpaper.

She knows what magic is –
the stress we're under.

*

Saturday's child is still growing into her eyes
(lamps above her chin, a frog's eyes surfacing

the muds of winter).
She can't help what she does and doesn't see –

salting away what she sees
inside her.

*

Sunday's child knows what blasphemy is
and where the devil's grave.

He makes the lovely graves
of long grass and speedwell.

The Ambition

after Rabelais

The tide being out, I had to traipse through dehydrated eelgrass and the chopped warm salad of the shallows, and then the Atlantic breached me part by part.

If my knees knocked it was two flints striking
My skin shagreen
My thorax a corset compressed rib by rising rib
My fingerprints finely-carved trilobites of the shore
My fine motor skills as good as any butterwort's
My nail-beds pale flukes: lemon soles or witches
My blood a thick slow scrawl of crude
If seals mobbed the shallows, it was only for my liver
If my kidneys complained, they were Bert and Ernie
My throat a maypole for eel-grass
My retinas red rags to bulls
A raw kebab, my vertebrae strung on the spinal cord
My nose and ears sympathetic remora
My pigtail a withered stipe or shaw
My moles and freckles rising spores
If I floated it was spatch-cock, trussed on the swell
If I expressed myself well, it was liquids and vowels
My musculature like dispersing cirrus
My sweat-glands like mud-buried lugworms
My children a cloud of clumped alfabeti
My urine a strong, hot tisane

If my knuckles were cracked, it was for their chilled marrow
My lips and tongue seasoned by an infinite cruet
My sphincters the knots in a balloon poodle
My brain-pan a shovel of quenched ash
My cerebellum a bait-ball
The full moon the most serious in a season of crushes
My slack my hammock
My plankton my inattention
My ghost pots my amnesia for names and faces
My luciferins my name in lights
My name sticks and sinking stones
My littoral my high-disclosure zone
My breadcrumb sponge my ephemeral path home

To be benthic

for Don Paterson

like the foram
in the midnight zone

which does one thing
which makes one thing

remote sun anglepoised
as he sweats out his test

attention coalesced
on a single opus

Hydra

for D & S & F & A & L

Were we like a plough, ancient or modern,
or a plough like us – as you taught us to *dell*,

to dig as digging used to be done
the four of us side by side, and moving as one

along each new row and down the fallowed yard?
Straining to turn the chunked soil,

we intermittently fell into a genius rhythm:
trod the spade-heads, and teetered while you cut

the corner of the clod; raising our blades
in the fissure to turn the dead weight

of it together and then striking
the same, rolled clod in unison

with spades honed to a thin, ragged edge,
as cobras with their hoods spread dash

from the same knot of muscle.
Just as often I whacked one

of you with my hip or arse or our hat-brims clashed
or the spade just missed the hand that darted

into turned earth for docken root or shards of lim
or we eyed Foula, distant

in blue haze, and panted, or hosed the pig,
who shuddered the water from her curling bristles

and tacked about her park. We filled our hats
at the tap and worked on with earlobes dripping,

while the dryness washed down from our first row,
the turned roots parching in the sun,

until it was done,
in the cooling of the light.

Manure

for Morris and Lorna

Your dung-heap is perfect
(your croft the neatest in
Valhalla with the most
dapper grass) – perfectly

square in its corrugate
pen, with the wine-dark
grain of slow-cured ham,
an oily cube of opium.

I bet your spades are sharp.
You know how to look
after things. Mine's blunt,
sighing into the dung,

from its blade crumbles
the rich wafer. Dense
as a black hole, a quantum
spade-full fills each bag: the

burgundy, the Chateau Neuf-
de-Poop. I swing it like a
wrecking ball, over a fence
more tuned than strung.

Olick

for Keith

Arriving on newspaper
like a headline, in very
clean jeans and bloody
yellow boots: you,

feeding me through the
brief autumn as if I'm
entitled to a tithe of ling,
by virtue of biding in

Babby Hunter's hoose.
You've already gutted it.
Half-cod, half-eel:
olick fill the sink – stiff

hoops of smoggy bullion,
the spine so thick
that every blow of the
cleaver makes the dead

fish gasp. And isn't it
always feast or famine?
All night I ingot fish,
stockpile fish.

Water comes to the boil.

The loose livers
liquidate their good oil.

Da Coall

tae-girse, tormentil; /whitna tapestry for a killin field
– Christine De Luca, 'Da Coall'

Sundew

Does this place look to you
like the cusp of never
and nothing and nowhere?

Look down into the encampment
of the blanket bog. It flushes
as it sweats out round-leaved sundew:

gold-panning, double-
bunking, a mass of dew-
blinged eyes. They just spread

their sticky fingers to get back
in the black; close them
on a fortune of tiny flies.

Butterwort

Forget the day's *eye*.
The bog's an erogenous zone
baroqued by a million Gaudís –
wave upon wave of zany
nano-blooms proffering
their tender meat-and-two-
veg to the air. I've fallen
to my knees again not five
minutes from home: first,
the boss of Venusian leaves
that look more like they docked
than grew; a sappy nub;
violet bell; the minaret
of purpled bronze. And
milkwort, gentian, asphodel,
a Sistine ceiling of flowers.

Spring Squill

What does spring cost
the blanket bog?
The thin-skinned

rabbit knows –
tunnelling down into
mantel and core –

dead-end of
earth-fast rock –
starve/rest –

and surface
here,
very, heart

hammering, in a streaming
mirage of *scilla verna*, migraine
of tormentil.

Puffballs

for Lotte Glob

You Mork eggs –
you Finns, you eyeless
Día de Muertos
skulls – how
do you and your
nation grow?

Are you
peripatetic,
rolled about the cliffs
until the music stops,
when each lets down
a frail plait?

Or the moon
herds you up
through the mold
like little white bulls,
forcing the wall
of the *kyunnen's*
burrow

•

When I wake on the cliff, with heart beating down
on the thin dungy soil, and waves seeming to break
inside me, I would just like to know what lies
between belly and bedrock. I know how securely

the cliff clasps you and that to touch
with lips is like nuzzling a kneecap.
To snack on you – sheepish – where you grow
is like eating *löragub*, sea-haze, expanding foam.

To sniff your socket in the grass
is to recall some humid porch of the body.
To explore it with my tongue
very saucy, grass tickling my chin.

Your tanned hide is already
the colour of a bog burial's skin, bronzed
and thin, half-hollow now, but tough but
perforated neatly by a raindrop

•

and you live
to sing to blurt

your spore-mass
from your ragged

moue!
O pepperpot

lift up
your voice! –

for the wind
to broadcast,

like smoke,
like spice.

The Plinky-Boat

the present is a fine line [. . .] *a puff of air would destroy it*
– Gaspar Galaz, 'Nostalgia de la Luz'

Something near to true
night-darkness. The children
are playing the Plinky-Boat –
a xylophone made
from a reclaimed yoal –
built for flexibility in a coarse
sea, you can tell it fledged
with ease, just blushed
from boat to instrument,
transpiring streams
of these hoarse night-
notes. For its copper pipes
are cut to breadth exactly
so the boat's beam is
its sotto voce and two rills
of rising pitch run into
the harmonic of each
hinnyspot – where
the boards of gunwales
and stem flow together.
I don't know what it is
about this place that things
metaflower so readily
into their present selves.

The instrument's a boat,
the notes unresonant
and scales of thin light
swarm over the pipes
from the boys' headtorches.
Perhaps we heard seals
broaching in the harbour
as they answered the girls
' hand clapping game –
I doubt they moaned
in their haunted wise –
here was everything –
words lost, as I'm trying
to say, their echo, that
yodel into past and future.
The poem wouldn't exist,
but we couldn't stay.

The Jellyfish

You cast into the wind.

There were no fish
surely there were no fish anywhere
just the shore ringed

with moon jellies
a violet nebula stranded and spun
by the current.

I said *I think I'm a jinx.*
You said *I think you might be.*
You picked a hook

from a little sillock's gill
chucking it back to cast
again. The mild carousel

of jellyfish
plied the surface from
the open sea

almost
inaudibly rising
and falling

from Definitions

The Bonfire

There's no closer reading than a fire's – rubbing its face over verso and recto working its way outwards from the heart and wringing off each page – 'I want you', 'I'm sorry sweetheart' – gorgeous cirrhosis of each doublespread – to tumble on the wind – in gobbits of claret and violet flame.

The Cat

is sleeping very deeply now it's spring been off his head hunting rabbits all night, in the far out stones and discoball eyes of the clifftop crö. His days a kind of stoned remission: heart-beat irregular, muscles leaping violently in sleep. The wet bracelet of his mouth unlatched; chattering a little; his eyelids half-open. His furry buffers nicely spread all about him; nicely buffered by fat and fur all round.

The Word 'Died'

It's a cliff-sided stack: sheer, almost an island. A human can't stand upon that high, tilted pasture but life crowds its cliffs: sheep and nesting maas, the waste-not plants of heath and moor. You hear the waves breaking but can't see them. You shrink down into yourself as you reach the edge: getting your head around where you are. It's marvellous. It's aweful. It is always on. Like a massive *and* unfolding its wings, and mantling. It was here all along, reached by Shirva and the derelict mills; turf sweating in the hot, midgy smirr.

The Mackerel

At once, the three hooks chime. The skin is as supple as the skin on boiled milk and the eye a hard, roundel pane. It is or it isn't wormy, it tastes of hot blood and earth, tastes of long-awaited rain, winter lightning and summer thunder. Heart-throb; mud-coloured; the cooked flesh is tarnish. The oatmeal crisp. It tastes of steak, it tastes of cream.

The Parents

are on the pale brisk longbusy birdbrushed billows of the equinoctial sea. Without them is a long, unhappy holiday. Who else gives a shit about your shitty knee? You're breathless at the thought of them all-night on the sea. Blithely they step into its bright pale machinery. They make mandalas of quartz and limpet-shells, hide cash under a hairbrush, vanish with their luggage as pixies might. The pillows squared to each other. The sheets pulled tight.

The Puffballs

Somebody's watching. Two toughened eyeballs propped behind you on the turf.

The Puffin

A tangled marionette, strings of jerked sinew. Summer's end,
the derelict burrow, a ring of dirty down. An arabesque of smelly
bone, meat for flies and the darling turf. The head may be full
of meat; the large beak, faded: a Fabergé egg.

The Waxcaps

Someone was carried across this field, bleeding steadily.

Five Mackerel

for Mary

Here's something
we can begin
to get our heads
around unlike

her summer
leaving

your kitchen
the unexpected
  mackerel

potato salad
with spring onion
big chunks
of apple

the hot, spitting fish
split easily
with the back
of the knife

opened
along its rig
the pinbones
drawn out.

And then
for the contrast
the boiled chunks
with just a *scar*

of vinegar
almost
a dessert
of fish

the cold tap
run over them.

The Moult

Stay out of the sun:
we can all see you. Stop picking fights
above your weight. We've this high

golden bowl of heather and moss
company of whaups and cries and
mutters in the wind; the long

draught of islands

and blinding sea.

Shelter in the hoodoos and pluck
your fur – fine smelt caught on heather
and shining reeds –

ruing it as I do, this flying
gleaming floss snatched back
and spent by the wind.

Freeze when the sunlight hits you

you're not invisible. Scratch off

your dreamcoat of silver money.
Rest downwind in the sun. Run
double-jointed when the valley dims.

from Hairst

The sun reaches the back wall.
My sparrow nib tosses aside
wet leaves of shadow

*

Moon a bashed swede.
I cut a way into the prickly core
of the dogroses.

Black bouquets: hollow stalks, rattling pods.
The secateurs are broken: their blades cross-
bill, twisted out of true

*

Ringing unanswered on the cliff,
like an old black bakelite
phone, the raven

*

Gate like a chapped mouth,
that the wind picks
and peels, gate that droops outwards

like a broken wing and utters
until it's empty, giving
and giving

*

To know your place:
a doorstep amongst the floating
islands

*

The wind's always got to be the dame
in a ten-gallon hat
fake fruit and flowers overflowing

*

The children shout *I'm dead,*
lying on their backs
on wet concrete; leap up;

cross the playground heel
-to-toe, hoist the blue gym mats
to catch the gale

A Very Circular Song

At the brink of the cliff the boy on the quadbike
goes round and around the crag at the gyo,
the bull in the ring of his own making
and the halfmoon Nissen huts are lit
and their doors rolled back
on bright trowie-halls in the hill.

And the wind turns like a great water-wheel
coming from the north to pad briefs
on the line with pudenda of the wind
which someone would need to take in
before the next shower, or leave them drenched
to dry again. And gales are followed

by rare, clear days and steady, cold nights,
like tankers to tow the next gale in.
More or less crucially, across the isles,
these acts exceed themselves, like trout-mouthings;
the cement mixer baying at the daylight moon,
the leg-hobbled, baby-faced Texel tup

scoring a dial in the sodden yard
as the boy on the quad goes round
and around the same crag
tearing the trembling bog with his tyres,
the headlight and the tail-light
at the brink of the gyo.

from *The Stone Age*

After Vestey's Well

for Jock

I raised the lid on myself. Rain jellied
what was down there – a toad –
swaying on his marks like a sprinter
on the block. When I reached for him, he bulbed;
          between him, me, the bar,
an oscillating current flowed.

I pried this chilled pat running with rain.
He swallowed and tried to swallow himself down –
we eddied in the rain, gulping smoke
from the bar, where there'd be wine and spinies
in parsley butter, whisky and Yes-talk.
As if it were a joystick

he curled his digits
around the crown of my finger,
which released him into thick, wet grass.

He front-crawled slowly
through its stiff, black waves.

Granny Whose Gaze

Granny whose gaze
was very much the moon
half-full is in her green
coat in the holly wood.

Granny whose gaze was
very much the moon
half-full is not far off,
second rung of the

the stepladder up
in the boughs of the
baking apple tree.
Her gaze dwindling

through its last quarter,
Granny declared with
unusual apology *I don't*
like to see the new moon

through glass at least
I tend to think it's
unlucky for me, turning
from her reflection

in her clear dusk cardigan –
because she couldn't abide
to be idle, and so prized
the days she got a lot

done

Wild Garlic

it was

a great trip, though the come-down
was this terrible thirst
for rain, my
mouth a limed
hollow, and all night
the garlic-loud glade
repeated on me in psychedelic
gusts: the forest floor was
a crackling
sea, and the sea was on fire
with glossy, green flames.

A hundred limbs did rot
and drop from loose sleeves
of moss –

a civilisation
of straight lines fell – deleted by *li*,

and I heard the bark of my long-
lost deep-green feral Gran –

keep your trap shut
about this, breathe not a word
to anyone

Skunk Cabbage

I have no idea where I comes
to an end. Perhaps in walls I frantically throw
up, hands flachtering like birds between
the stones   or in skin touchy as an
electric fence   and when you
cross this moat of oily water,
to plant your foot on the
welcome mat of my
liver, I burp
out the naked truth
like a novelty doorbell, or
something spouting from

a vegetal gland: a
rattlesnake
pistil, waxy-white,

sheathed
in a fountain
of indigenous
leaves –

Umbrella

Thirty years ago, as this poem began, I thought people speaking another language were like people talking under umbrellas. Now wardens are out clearing the flood-traps, and gutter and hill run like a river, in little surges like rills of clear pleasure; and drops pop the fabric between the vanes, as if all I can throw up between me and the rain is the bivouac of my own eardrum.

On the threshold of the caff, I fold the umbrella to a long, dripping dart. The customers keep tracking in rain, splashing like sparrows in talk and clatter. Three women: three wells of standing water. One saying very calmly, 'one minute you're laughing, the next you're bawling your eyes out.' And another, 'but life has to go on, doesn't it?'

I open your book, to weather the present storm in its shelter. From time to time, no urgency whatsoever, a woman mops the slick from the floor. Now I see I'm the one under the umbrella, and everyone else is standing in the rain: gilled, they swim through its drenching blether and never look like they're drowning –

Oyea

It always seems like you shout
your feelings like a town crier,
and I proclaim my feelings like
a town crier, and folk don't so

much share as ring out their
feelings like crowds of town
criers, turning this way and
that, throwing their chins to

the sky to toll with a strong
downward clang the feelings:
summons we perpetually serve
on each other. As if at the edict

of some abdicating king, perhaps
a stark-bollock-naked one, his
lieutenant standing nude in the
king's name too, Armistice

and christening, the alarum
peal: I feel! I feel! I feel! I feel!

Dolmen

Standing stone, let's
talk about
You! Who knows
how deep this grief goes
down – with your thick waist
and whalebone skirt –
          goodnessknows
how deep and wide –
twinkling modestly with
garnet, feldspar –

whiffing
(faintly) of bruised
mushroom.

Now, we learnt
in school about Deep
Time. Six

o'clock shadow: lichen.
Pouringdownlikeporridge:
lichen. But humankind
are brief, soft

fireworks, prone
to go off at a moment's
notice. Are we even speaking the
same language? Urgently

we hammer at your
boarded-up window,
          rattle and try

your grittygrey door!

Hardanger Fiddle & Nyckelharpa

So help me – I would rather write a song,
a wordless song for the
strings of the North –

Hardanger fiddle and

Nyckelharpa –
like jewels hewn in flaxen wood,
keys a delicate overbite.

Elfish devices in mother-of-pearl like
nights the sea calms
paler than the sky – short bow light

enough to touch the nerves of the North

fretful in a shiver
of sympathetic strings

feeling in their flat chests
how close the night has moored to silence. Bored

wind gowling in the bars of the
gate, purr of surge when the night
is still, so help me – write

a song of unsettling
grace, perhaps an old folk-dance
in a weird time-signature,

a gawky
waltz, a
lonely march: gone off at a tangent,

popped back to say   *it was just*

a random thought –

an interrupted cadence –
a whistle under the breath –

Shadow

So this is where I left my
shadow – italic,
underweight – stashed
like a tushkar in the

corner of your kitchen.
What in god's name have
you been feeding it?
Dark plates of hashed

hellery, like pie for birds;
long winter of the berried
dark – I can't believe my
delinquent shadow – fat

and glossy – full as a tick –
muddy shadow running amok –
shagging this bright rock –
the hill – snaps mockingly to

attention when I cry
Heel! Welling bottomless
at my foot – roosts in my
clavicle – opens its throat.

You press on me the leash
of my shadow. Say, *Open*
the granite wardrobe of your breast.
Fold in your shadow

like a warm, winter coat –

Rhubarb

In winter, low
tide comes to the rhubarb
box and bares
stiff reefs of coral

, midsummer – we rustle rhubarb, lean
and feral, from its driftwood corral. It's
late

        but I'm not tired at all, as you
yearn over the rotting fence – I say
   Careful! You'll be
man overboard! then you plunge like a

pearl-fisher into creaking billows,
 clipping thin petioles with
your special knife

. In the west, the sky is pink as rhubarb. You say
you're not that into
sunsets.

We hike to the far cliffs
as if the night will never fall, my
bouquet of rhubarb

weirdly heavy, like
an armful of water . . . millefiore. I say,

They called him the Rhubarb Rustler. You say
everything's early this year.

You say, the rain is good when it's soft.
You say, it's fine
to have children to borrow

. Now

a bird begins
to whistle. The rusty ears creak
and swivel. Dim green of the

hill is yawning
visible and the little-voiced
dawn will soon be audible – and

   did I say how late it is? In
the East, the sky is pink as rhubarb. So

we trim, at both ends, these
lean, sour, freckled stems,
and I say

   I'm just
         so tired –

Swans

Sound travels so far on the quiet evenings especially

in mist –

the human cough of sheep –

the graveyard gate with its quiet hinge.

On a still day you hear the beat of their wings –

something like the creaking of oars –

a longboat rowed from the sky's north shore –

the hoarse cry of the oarsmen –

Rockpool

Above the rockpool
everything is tilt or

rough, glazed in
weed like afterbirth

the sharp rocks
starry as the

domes of Istanbul
seedling barnacles

streaming down
the gutters of

the mosques
of the limpets

like falling stars.
This is no place

to show up
without a shell

all that protects us
from the press

of heaven –

Nudibranch

I ease my naked body down
into the rockpool's closet, clinging
to the vertical rocks with my soles,
hanging a moment
before I let myself fall   slowly
as a dim slip that shrugs off
its hanger in a deep, green changing room,
air shouting silently from my struck
lungs, I would try on
the old clothes to
see if they still fit. Dropping
to the velveted floor the seizing
onesie of brillo hair, the sweat-sheath
that horripilates with urchinous
buttons – each breaking wave
dousing me of costume,
comfortably
divested of my name.

Perhaps still some permeable
notion of self –

arabesques
of albumen –

prongs subliming
to tender flame

condensing
down to antlers

and weed and warm and
warm and

weed –

Limpet

Stop, now you're
home, and consider
what that feels like –
don't stop, continue

to whirl, an introvert
tornado, across the
flooded rockpool
in an ease of gypsy

skirts – cyclonic,
high and wet. This
is not a thing
to sit tight upon –

locked to your home-
scar against the
migraine of the waves –
this rebate will wait

that you can spin home to
like cup to saucer –
matching every chip
in your shell to its

own rocky rostrum.
Clamp down –
turn the key of
yourself in the lock

of yourself, fasten –
with a hundred
infinitesimal
mortices –

Ert-fast

I midwife a hundred
rocks in a day: red
rocks, glistening
like anvils.

Each
must be delivered
in its own way, uncleaving
root-veined fascias –

with shocking noise they
broach the light – red-
cheeked and muddy, marred
and birth-marked,
leaving in sucking soil

the imprint of their
darling faces.

I prise the sticking
children, backbreaking work –
but no poor me, although

I've been a missionary
while you raised your
one or two –

I have this
consolation of
strong and silent types,

my hundred
quiet ones,

that take to talking
late and slow –

Strimmer

Strimmer, you butcher,
you-as-soul are the hardest to
imagine. A poor soul, a kind soul, a
good soul – easy! – soul a deep
ladle, soul a ladder. How
intimately we tangle with our
tools – grafting them into
our brains like prostheses – I'm
appalled by your skinny neck,
thrusting the flat howl of your face
into the meadow's tangle,
screaming at stinging nettle, couch-
grass, clover; sending flying
little moth-scrap-souls.
I can't find a thing to
admire in you –
thrash-metal strap-on whose
obsession with yield makes
yielding impossible –
   stumbling
onward in evangelical
fury, roaring
your hateful rhetoric. All small
voices drowned out in the carnage, the fresh
green blood
flying in my face –

Nettles

You tell me *the hope is the worst*, and
I say yes, like nettles, the way they
seize hold of the soil's dark meat.
Out at midnight with the garden fork,

I mean to eradicate hope, like an
amputation of the nervous system,
I will parse its searing sea-ferns clear
of my body. But as I haul on this

red-hot rope, what I hear is the
last-chance clanking of a drawbridge,
and as I drag this scalding root,
each and every snapped-off

shoot spouts its manyheads of
hope,

        and (to misquote)

many waters   cannot
quench hope –

First Draft

for Janet

We drew a house in the wind with string, just
drafted it out with string & wind, & rocks
the isle is consonant in to pin down this
intangible thing. The measuring tape tacked

across the wind, bulging to accommodate what
a life might bring; the house dragged south;
like a tent or full sail, a lively haul in a purse
seine. Correcting its course, I thought – with

rocks & string, & blackbird's song & thirsty
wind – this almost looks like home – then
struck the tent and furled the sail; kicking rocks;
winding up – a rambling thought – the orange

string. & was glad to see the house undone –
& I still feel its tug against the wind –

ACKNOWLEDGEMENTS

Some of these poems appear in a different order than in the collections where they were first published. Titles in italics in the contents list are unpublished pieces written at the same time as the collections in which they now appear. 'The Jellyfish' was previously published in *Byssus* as 'The Jinx'.

Poems from the collections *Almanacs* (2005) and *Nigh-No-Place* (2008) are reprinted with kind permission of Bloodaxe Books.

A version of 'To be benthic' was published in *Things Unspoken / Things Unseen* (ed. Bevan and Roe), commissioned by Anne Bevan.

'Wild Garlic' was published in *The Yale Review*.